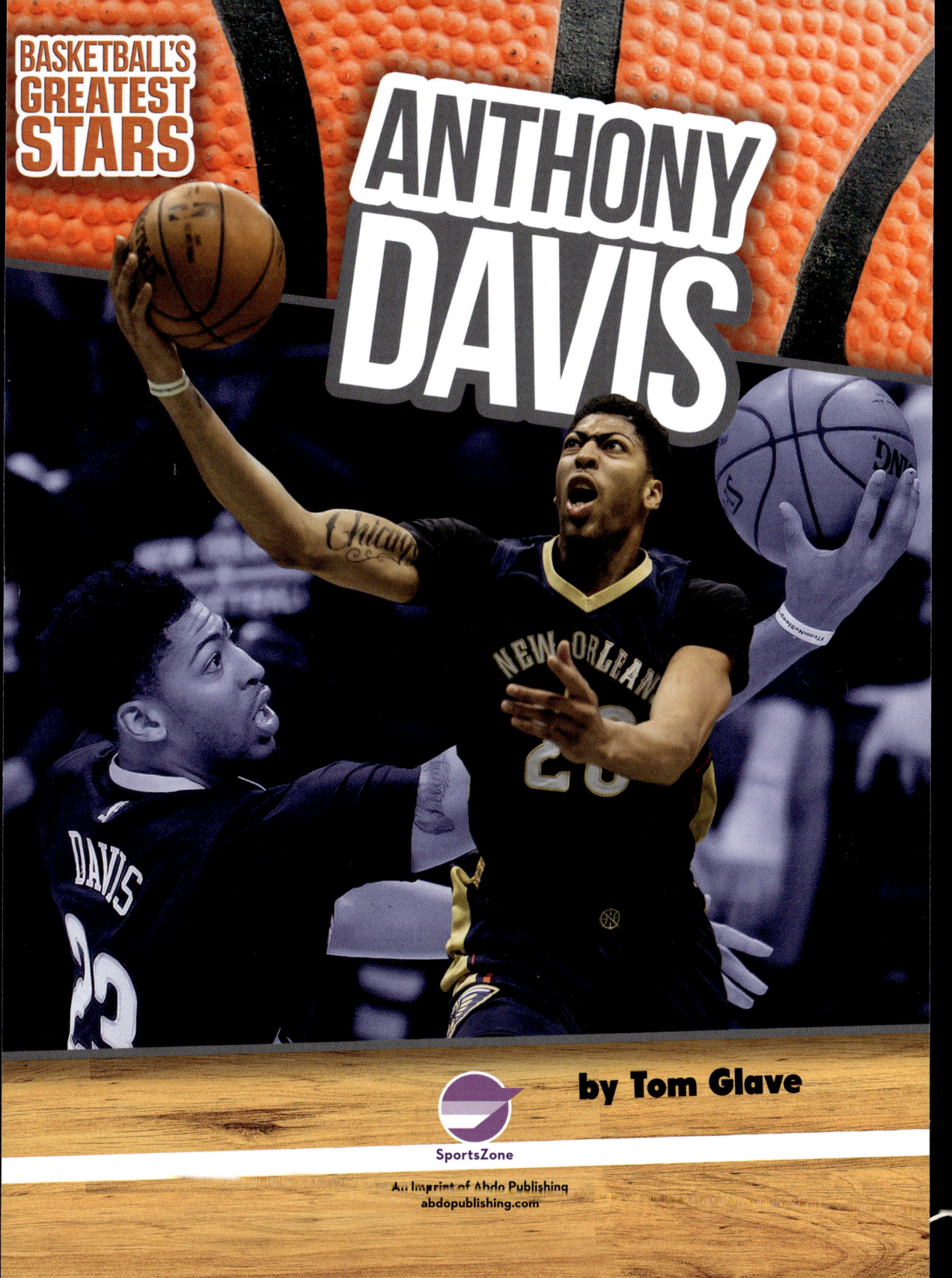

BASKETBALL'S GREATEST STARS

ANTHONY DAVIS

by Tom Glave

SportsZone
An Imprint of Abdo Publishing
abdopublishing.com

abdopublishing.com

Published by Abdo Publishing, a division of ABDO, PO Box 398166, Minneapolis, Minnesota 55439. Copyright © 2017 by Abdo Consulting Group, Inc. International copyrights reserved in all countries. No part of this book may be reproduced in any form without written permission from the publisher. SportsZone™ is a trademark and logo of Abdo Publishing.

Printed in the United States of America, North Mankato, Minnesota
092016
012017

 THIS BOOK CONTAINS RECYCLED MATERIALS

Cover Photos: Tom Lynn/AP Images, foreground; Hector Acevedo/Cal Sport Media/AP Images, background
Interior Photos: Tom Lynn/AP Images, 1 (foreground); Hector Acevedo/Cal Sport Media/AP Images, 1 (background); Stephen Lew/Cal Sport Media/AP Images, 4-5; Carlos Osorio/AP Images, 6, 7, 8-9; Brian Kersey/AP Images, 10-11; Rick Bowmer/AP Images, 12, 13, 22-23; Jonathan Bachman/Cal Sport Media/AP Images, 14-15; David J. Phillip/AP Images, 16; Mark Cornelison/The Lexington Herald-Leader via AP Images, 17; Eric Gay/AP Images, 18; Bill Kostroun/AP Images, 19; Reed Saxon/AP Images, 20-21; Alvaro Barrientos/AP Images, 24-25; Stephen Lew/Icon Sportswire/AP Images, 26; Marcio Jose Sanchez/AP Images, 27; Jason Bean/Las Vegas Review-Journal/AP Images, 28; Tyler Kaufman/AP Images, 29

Editor: Todd Kortemeier
Series Designer: Laura Polzin

Publisher's Cataloging-in-Publication Data
Names: Glave, Tom, author.
Title: Anthony Davis / by Tom Glave.
Description: Minneapolis, MN : Abdo Publishing, 2017. | Series: Basketball's greatest stars | Includes index.
Identifiers: LCCN 2016945483 | ISBN 9781680785449 (lib. bdg.) | ISBN 9781680798074 (ebook)
Subjects: LCSH: Davis, Anthony, 1993- --Juvenile literature. | Basketball players--United States--Biography--Juvenile literature.
Classification: DDC 796.323 [B]--dc23
LC record available at http://lccn.loc.gov/2016945483

CONTENTS

A SHINING STAR 4

GROWING IN THE GAME 10

BECOMING THE BEST 14

GOING PRO 18

IMPROVING IN THE NBA 24

Timeline 30
Glossary 31
Index 32
About the Author 32

A SHINING STAR

Anthony Davis proved himself to be a defensive star early in his National Basketball Association (NBA) career. The New Orleans Pelicans' star power forward showed off his offense on February 21, 2016 against the Detroit Pistons.

Pelicans center Omer Asik got hurt early in the game. With Asik out, Davis had to carry most of the load under the basket. He worked hard to get good shots and dominated the post.

Anthony Davis scored 34 points against the Philadelphia 76ers on February 19, 2016.

FAST FACT

Davis is well known for his "unibrow." His eyebrows appear to be connected in the middle. He trademarked the sayings "Fear the Brow" and "Raise the Brow" before the 2012 NBA Draft.

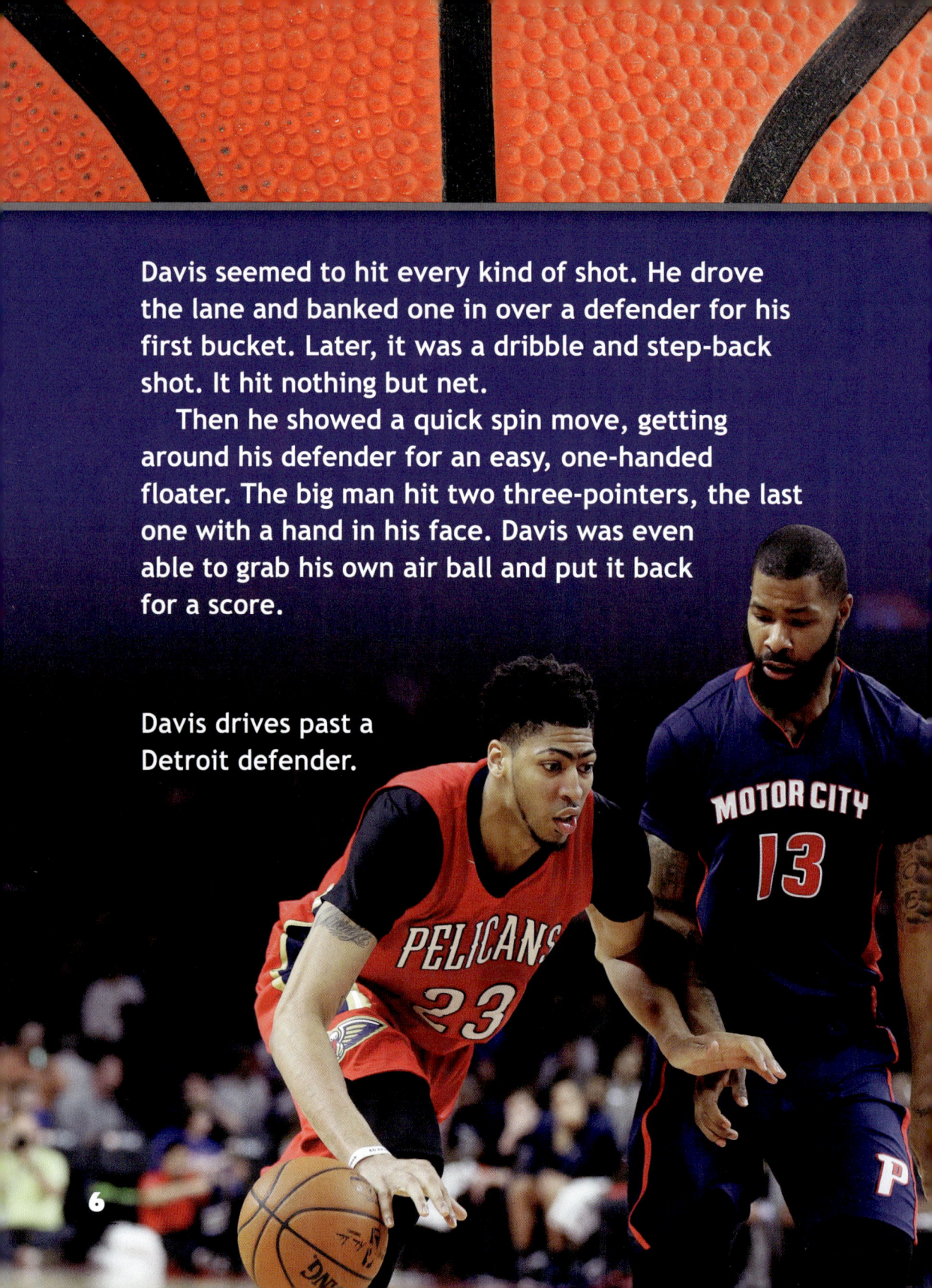

Davis seemed to hit every kind of shot. He drove the lane and banked one in over a defender for his first bucket. Later, it was a dribble and step-back shot. It hit nothing but net.

Then he showed a quick spin move, getting around his defender for an easy, one-handed floater. The big man hit two three-pointers, the last one with a hand in his face. Davis was even able to grab his own air ball and put it back for a score.

Davis drives past a Detroit defender.

Davis throws down a dunk against Detroit.

Davis's teammates celebrate his 59-point game by pouring water on him.

Davis topped his career high of 43 points with a jumper from the elbow midway through the fourth quarter. Then he broke the team scoring record with a driving dunk five minutes later.

Davis finished with 59 points. At 22, Davis became the youngest NBA player to score that many points in one game. It was the kind of game Pelicans fans wanted to see from their young star. Davis also grabbed 20 rebounds as the Pelicans beat the Pistons 111-106.

FAST FACT

Only two other players have recorded 55 points and 20 rebounds in an NBA game. They are Hall of Famers Shaquille O'Neal and Wilt Chamberlain.

GROWING IN THE GAME

Anthony Davis was born March 11, 1993, in Chicago. He is one minute older than his twin sister, Antoinette. His older sister, Iesha, played basketball at Daley College in Chicago.

Davis was an oversized infant and his family called him "Fat Man." The nickname stuck through most of his youth. Davis' parents are both over 6 feet (1.8 m) tall. But he passed them up by the time he was a junior in high school.

FAST FACT

Davis was 6-foot-10 (2.1 m) as a senior but had the skills of a guard. He learned to rebound and block shots after he grew. He also passes and shoots well for a big man.

Davis, *32*, made the McDonald's All American Game in his senior season as one of the best high school players in the country.

Davis attended Perspectives Charter High School. It was known more for academics than sports. It didn't even have its own gym. Davis didn't focus on basketball at first. He wanted to get good grades and go to college.

Davis was a guard when he started playing basketball. He went through workouts with his cousins and uncle. Davis grew eight inches between his sophomore and senior years of high school. Soon he started to dominate on the court.

Davis, *10*, played for Team USA in the Nike Hoop Summit game as a high school senior.

Davis takes a shot against the World Team at the Nike Hoop Summit. Team USA won, 92-80.

FAST FACT

Davis donated $65,000 to Perspectives Charter High School after his first season in the NBA. The money was used to build an outdoor basketball court. The new court replaced a portable hoop in the parking lot.

BECOMING THE BEST

Anthony Davis played on a summer team before his senior year. He showed his skills at tournaments, and college coaches started to notice.

Davis grew three inches that summer. He was 6-foot-10 (2.1 m) when school started. Davis averaged 32 points, 22 rebounds and seven blocks during his senior season. He won several awards and was a finalist for national player of the year. His great play attracted lots of scholarship offers. He chose the University of Kentucky.

Kentucky fans were thrilled when Davis chose to play for the Wildcats.

FAST FACT

Davis started his senior year with a bang. Many fans and scouts were there to watch him. He wowed them by nailing a fadeaway three-pointer on one of the game's first plays.

Davis led Kentucky in scoring and had 186 blocks as a freshman. He leaped high to block a shot in the final seconds of a December 2011 win against North Carolina.

The Wildcats won the national championship in April. Davis had six points, 16 rebounds and six blocks in the title game. His defense gave Kansas trouble all night. He forced a turnover in the final 30 seconds to seal the win.

Davis helps cut down the nets after Kentucky made it to the Final Four.

Davis blocks a last-second shot to preserve a win against North Carolina.

FAST FACT

Davis received several national awards in his one year at Kentucky. He was named the nation's best player and the best player at the Final Four.

GOING PRO

Anthony Davis decided to enter the NBA Draft after his freshman season. Scouts liked Davis's athletic ability and his dominating defense. He showed he could shoot jumpers and throw down big dunks.

Davis stood 6-foot-11 (2.1 m) before the draft with an armspan of 7 feet, 6 inches (2.3 m). Teams also liked that Davis helped his teammates. He did what he could to help the team win, even if he wasn't scoring. The New Orleans Hornets used the first pick of the 2012 draft to select Davis.

Davis got to play with Team USA in the 2012 Olympics before making his NBA debut.

Davis greets NBA Commissioner David Stern after being chosen first overall in the draft.

FAST FACT

Davis won a gold medal with Team USA at the 2012 Olympic Games in London, England. He averaged 3.7 points in limited action.

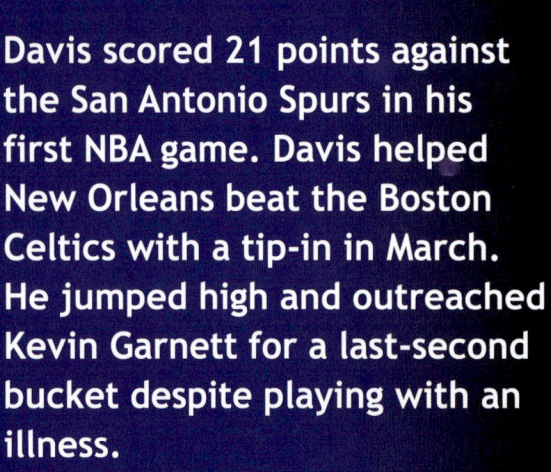

Davis scored 21 points against the San Antonio Spurs in his first NBA game. Davis helped New Orleans beat the Boston Celtics with a tip-in in March. He jumped high and outreached Kevin Garnett for a last-second bucket despite playing with an illness.

Davis averaged 13.5 points, 8.2 rebounds, and 1.8 blocks during his rookie season. His 20 double-doubles led all rookies.

FAST FACT

The Charlotte Hornets moved to New Orleans in 2002. In April 2013, they changed their name to the Pelicans. The Charlotte Bobcats took on the Hornets name.

Davis was named to the NBA All-Rookie Team in 2012-13.

Davis started his second season with two double-doubles. He blocked nine shots in a November win against Philadelphia and finished the year leading the NBA with 2.8 blocks per game.

Davis had 40 points and 21 rebounds in a win against Boston in March. He dominated the middle in overtime with six rebounds. A week later, he scored 30 points against the defending champion Miami Heat.

FAST FACT
Davis scored 10 points in his first NBA All-Star Game in 2014.

Davis stepped up his offense in his second season, averaging more than 20 points per game.

IMPROVING IN THE NBA

Anthony Davis hit big shots throughout the 2014-15 season. He made a game-winning layup against defending champion San Antonio in November. Davis capped a 41-point game with a buzzer-beating three-pointer against the Oklahoma City Thunder in February. He caught an inbounds pass and hung in the air before shooting between two defenders.

In March, Davis hit two clutch jumpers in the final minute to beat Detroit. He averaged 24.4 points per game on the season and helped New Orleans reach the playoffs.

In the summer before the 2014-15 season, Davis played for Team USA at the Basketball World Cup, helping win the gold medal.

FAST FACT

The Pelicans had to beat the San Antonio Spurs in their final game to make the playoffs. Davis beat the shot clock with a baseline jumper in the final minutes and sealed the win by blocking a driving layup.

The Pelicans were swept by the eventual NBA champion Golden State Warriors in Davis's first playoff series.

Davis had 35 points and a couple of big dunks in his first game but the Pelicans couldn't complete a late comeback. He put up 29 points in Game 3, but the Warriors rallied from a 20-point deficit to win.

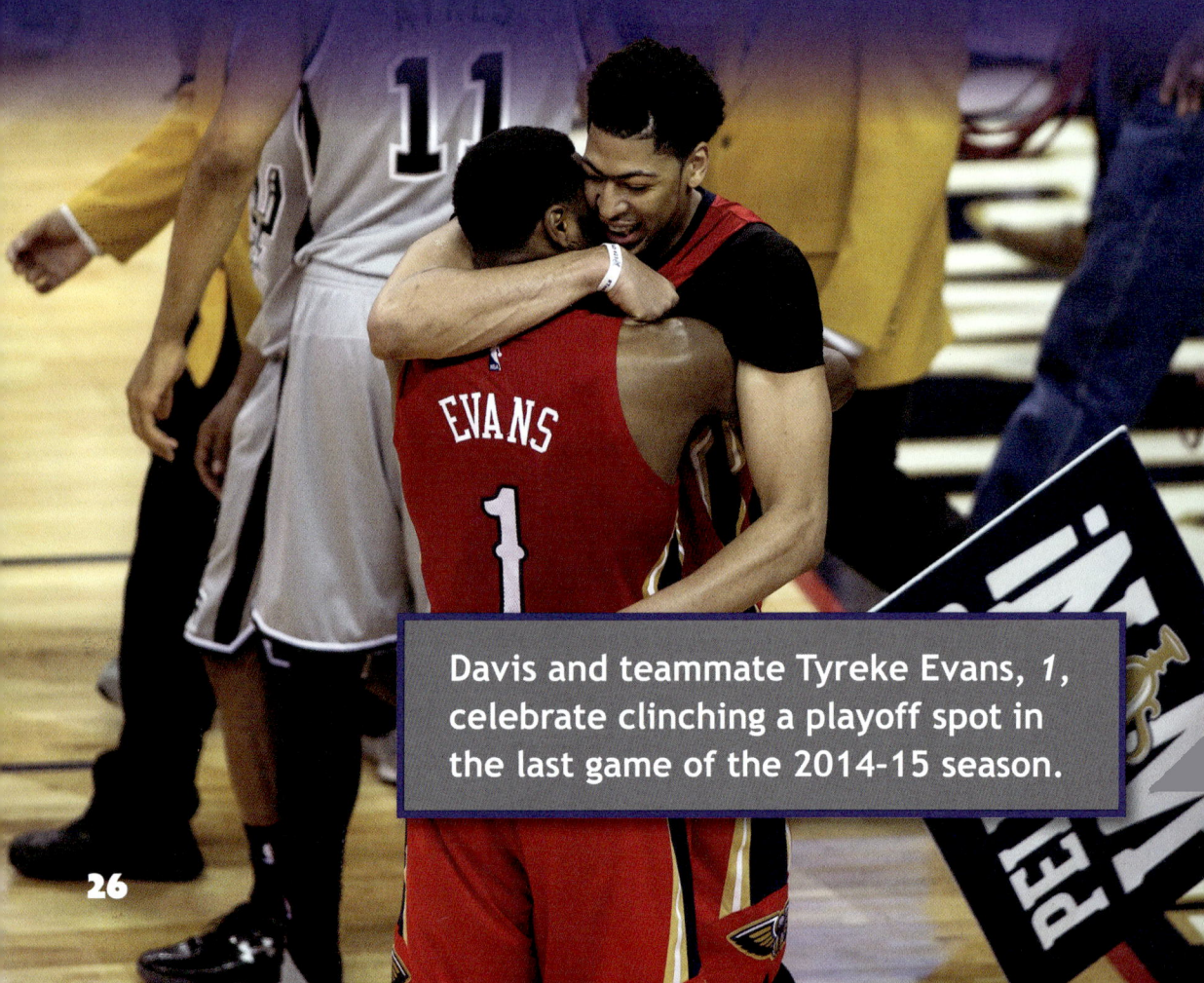

Davis and teammate Tyreke Evans, *1*, celebrate clinching a playoff spot in the last game of the 2014-15 season.

Davis slams home a dunk in his first career playoff game.

FAST FACT

Davis finished the 2014-15 season leading the NBA in blocked shots per game for the second time. He was named to the All-NBA First Team.

In 2015-16, Davis added a new skill to his game. After hitting only three three-pointers in his first three seasons, he nailed 35. He averaged 24.3 points per game. And he kept making highlight-reel dunks, like a two-hander against Charlotte in January. Davis caught an alley-oop and slammed it home with two seconds left to win the game.

But Davis's season was cut short because of injuries. He tried to play through it, but he wasn't effective. Pelicans fans hope he comes back better than ever and leads them back to the playoffs.

Davis's play and trademark unibrow make him a fan favorite for both Team USA and the Pelicans.

Davis acknowledges the crowd after being named to his third All-Star team in 2016.

FAST FACT

Davis made his third consecutive All-Star Game in 2015-16. He hit 12 of 13 shots for 24 points and added six rebounds.

TIMELINE

1993
Anthony Davis is born in Chicago on March 11, one minute before twin sister Antoinette.

2009
Davis grows three inches during the summer between his sophomore and junior years in high school.

2010
Davis signs with the University of Kentucky.

2012
Kentucky wins the college basketball national championship on April 2. Davis earns multiple Player of the Year awards.

2012
Davis is selected first overall by the New Orleans Hornets in the NBA Draft on June 28. He helps Team USA win the gold medal at the Olympics on August 12.

2014
Davis plays in his first NBA All-Star Game.

2015
Davis scores 31 points in a must-win game to put the Pelicans in the playoffs.

2016
Davis scores a career-high 59 points against Detroit.

GLOSSARY

AIR BALL
A shot that completely misses the basket.

CLUTCH
An important or pressure-packed situation.

DOUBLE-DOUBLE
When a player records a double-digit number of two statistics, such as points and rebounds.

FLOATER
A slow-moving shot that stays in the air longer before going in.

FRESHMAN
A first-year college player.

POST
The area around the basket where power forwards and centers usually play.

SCHOLARSHIP
Money given to a student to pay for education expenses.

SCOUT
A person whose job is to look for talented young players.

TRADEMARK
A unique or distinctive feature or characteristic.

INDEX

Asik, Omer, 4

Boston Celtics, 20, 22

Chamberlain, Wilt, 9
Charlotte Bobcats, 20
Charlotte Hornets, 20, 28
Chicago, Illinois, 10

Davis, Antoinette, 10
Davis, Iesha, 10
Detroit Pistons, 4, 6, 7, 8, 24

Evans, Tyreke, 26

Garnett, Kevin, 20
Golden State Warriors, 26

Miami Heat, 22

New Orleans Hornets, 18, 20
New Orleans Pelicans, 4, 8, 20, 24, 25, 26

O'Neal, Shaquille, 9
Oklahoma City Thunder, 24
Olympic Games, 18, 19

Perspectives Charter High School, 12, 13
Philadelphia 76ers, 4, 22

San Antonio Spurs, 20, 24, 25
Stern, David, 19

University of Kansas, 16
University of Kentucky, 14, 16, 17
University of North Carolina, 16, 17

ABOUT THE AUTHOR

Tom Glave learned to write about sports at the University of Missouri-Columbia and now writes about sports for newspapers, websites and books. He and his family live in Houston.